A Very Different Life

A Very Different Life

The Hardly-Boresome Adventures of an Obscure Woman

Margaret Heacock Knowles

Grand Cyrus Press

San Francisco

GRAND CYRUS PRESS, SAN FRANCISCO
www.GrandCyrusPress.com

ISBN 978-0-9790994-6-5
Library of Congress Control Number: 2012949254

Knowles, Margaret Heacock, 1881-1932

First Edition 2012

Cover design by Ann Marra

For information, contact
Grand Cyrus Press
1024 Sacramento St.
San Francisco, CA 94108-2003

www.GrandCyrusPress.com

Contents

Acknowledgments

Thanks to Jim Knowles for unearthing and preserving his grandmother's manuscripts and to his daughter Nancy Knowles and cousin Natalie Knowles Joranson for seeing the possibilities in their ancestress's stories.

Some people save things. Lots of things. Sometimes, they do not know what they are saving. The boxes containing these stories along with other family documents have been moved dozens of times in the past hundred years, finally sorted out by the grandson of the author.

To save a document, it is necessary only to keep the paper from harm. To save the stories themselves, it is necessary that they be read. The manuscripts of Marguerite (Margaret) Loraine Heacock Knowles came to me as photocopies of ninety-year-old carbon copies, some with penciled changes.

In preparing these stories for publication, I have not changed a single word, only corrected some spellings (though never updating vintage ones) and adjusted some rather haphazard punctuation where it was required for clarity. I have left the long strings of sentences separated by semicolons which were both the author's stylistic choice and a common feature of literature at the time. I have made all the penciled changes, deletions, and insertions on the copies when legible. However, when the author has written "expand on this," it is beyond my capacity to do so.

Eleanor Knowles Dugan

In 1905, a young wife arrived in a strange land to join her mining engineer husband. The challenges of her new life proved both exciting and dangerous. She recorded her domestic—and, later, historical—adventures with youthful enthusiasm and naïve bigotry in this series of engaging autobiographical essays. Her literary time capsules capture the attitudes and morés of the time while revealing a woman gently reared to live a life quite different from the difficult one she chose.

My First Day on Foreign Soil

Hot and disheveled from a long journey, I alighted from the train at *Estacion* San Gabriel. Holding my young first-born by the hand, I glanced about in surprise and dismay that there was no one there to greet me. No use to approach any of the dozen or so swarthy-faced men who lounged around as though they had nothing to do in life but to wait for something; I didn't know their language, nor they mine.

The station itself, not much larger than a boxcar, and a few adobe huts made up the sum total of this jumping off place with the Biblical name. Not even a bush softened the landscape; in every direction, the hot sand and cactus stretched out and met the horizon. There was nothing to do but to await developments as philosophically as possible. Before long, a cloud of sandy dust appeared in the distance, enveloping, as I surmised, the belated husband who had preceded us into the heart of this strange land.

After a brief respite for the four mules, we proceeded on the second lap of the immigration to our new home. I thought of

Estacion San Gabriel

my little grandmother and the forty-niners as I climbed into the canvas-covered wagon, and I recalled grandfather's tales of crossing the Mojave desert with the horses' tongues so swollen they almost choked and not a drop of water to allay their suffering. No such dramatic experience was in store for us, however; though exceedingly tiring, the ride was uneventful.

Just at sunset we came to the ore sheds at the foot of the mountain trail. Instructions had been given that horses were to be ready to carry us on the third and last lap of our travels, but due either to the faulty Spanish of my *esposo* or to the unhurried manner in which orders are executed in this land of *La Mañana* [the morrow], no one was awaiting us. The marvelous tropical sunset and the fresh, cooling breeze that invariably follows in the mountainous regions tempered our discomfort somewhat, but our small son refused to feast on Nature; weary and hungry, he cried for bread when there was nothing to offer but stones. Hours slipped by; in desperation we spread our sacks on the ground and attempted to sleep, but alas, that solace was denied

12

us. All the fleas in that section of the country had gathered here to make our acquaintance; a frightfully active, aggressive lot they were too. Product of the mid-west where men have rich, fragrant soil instead of hot, shifting sand beneath their feet, I remembered vaguely that there were such pests, but I associated them only with dogs. Here was a breed which attacked human beings, not singly or in pairs, but in battalions.

At four in the morning the relief came—horses, nourishment, and cool water. The hardships were quickly forgotten in the glories of that ride over the trail. The head of the family led the procession; I followed, and in the rear came the *mozo* [male servant] with our angel child. The mountain air was crisp at that hour; they had wrapped him in a red blanket and strapped him as only a native can, to the back of a burro. His body was bound stiffly upright; he looked for all the world like a chubby papoose. Though his head bobbed from side to side as we climbed over the rough places, he slept serenely through it all.

The rainy season was just drawing to a close, and the mountain-sides that were so nearly barren for many months of the year were now covered with a profusion of gorgeous wildflowers. Such flaming colors and such endless variety! I counted fifty different kinds within a small area. Cataracts trickled over the crevices in the rocks, and the scene was entrancing—a sharp contrast to the heat and barrenness of the cactus-covered sand plains.

Suddenly the procession halted, and the crack of a revolver broke the stillness. Another enemy of mankind had prepared a hostile reception. I shuddered at the sight of the big rattler which the watchful eye of our protector had discovered in the path, coiled ready to strike.

The home provided for the manager of *La Mina Purisima* was not built in the usual Mexican fashion with a court; the large, high rooms were strung along like links in a chain to snuggle into the narrow shelf dug out for them on the mountainside. The journey from one end to the other was quite a pilgrimage;

La Mina Purisima

it furnished me with daily exercise. Below us lay the mud huts of the miners while two thousand feet above over a rough and winding trail, men burrowed like gophers for the precious metal which is "the root of much evil." I was entirely alone when a *mozo* came running breathlessly to the door; his excited gestures, coupled with the words *"petaja"* and *"burro,"* revealed to me the fact that a dire catastrophe had befallen us; one of my huge trunks had rolled to the foot of the mountain carrying the little donkey with it. The heavy loads they carry are usually arranged on either side so that the weight is well balanced. A large, unyielding trunk was indeed an awkward cargo; probably in some narrow spot, the *mozo* had been compelled to step behind; under such a circumstance a bit of jutting rock would be sufficient to upset the equilibrium of the little burden bearer. I was frantic; I visualized the poor little wounded animal and my precious belongings scattered hither and thither, but here I was, with two thousand feet of stiff climbing between me and the *Señor*. Ignorant of the language, I could make no suggestions. There was nothing I could do, so I did it. The *mozo* at last understood my helplessness and vanished.

Imagine my amazement and my joy several hours later when the burro—apparently intact—walked jauntily into camp with the badly scratched but otherwise uninjured trunk still on his back. I had not misread the pantomime, but I was to learn that the cat with its proverbial nine lives has nothing on the burro— he has ninety and nine. You can neither starve nor kill him; he only dies of old age. As for the trunk—it was "Made in the U.S.A." which to my provincial soul was sufficient explanation of its durability.

And this was the end of an imperfect day—my first on foreign soil!

Many of the stories are portraits of women she met—exotic, funny, tragic women, each so different from anyone she had known during her sheltered Iowa upbringing. She grouped these encounters under the title Some Ships I Have Passed in the Night, *each narrative advancing her own story.*

Portrait: Chelina

Chelina was an institution; I was so informed by the owners of *La Mina Purisima* in whose domicile she had reigned supreme for many years, and I, as the wife of the new manager of the mine, was politely asked to regard her as such.

Little cause had they to fear that I would upset the domestic regime; I was a tenderfoot in this mountainous region of Old Mexico—young, inexperienced, provincial. To me, the *peóns* were individually and collectively potential bandits, but even they were not as terrifying as the old cook herself. For the first time in my life I believed in reincarnation; I felt certain that some evil spirit had taken possession of this little Indian mummy—she was a thousand if she was a day. Her beady eyes were like a snake's with neither pupil nor iris; just tiny glittering black balls which never under any circumstances revealed anything human when they furtively turned in my direction.

The kitchen had been added as an afterthought without the trouble of removing a glass window that separated it from the dining room. Sometimes I got up the courage to peek through the curtains, and what I saw was not exactly reassuring. On one occasion I discovered her squatted in the middle of the rough stone floor with the dishes piled all about her. She was bathing them in water thick with soap and grease, but, alas, they were not treated to the luxury of a rinse. During most of her waking hours she found solace in the midst of her labors in her cigarette. It was spellbinding to see how dexterously she could handle one while mixing biscuits or performing other tasks which would require both of the hands of just an ordinary mortal. In emergencies, the corn husk dainty was held securely between her toothless gums, and the ashes dropped where they listed. Lucky for the family when they missed the dough.

We were to learn to our sorrow that our ancient institution had a vice. One night, not long after our arrival, our peaceful slumbers were disturbed by piercing shrieks alternated with ribald laughter and tuneless singing. Chelina was saturated with *mezcal*.[1] Long shall I remember my struggles with the dinner on the following day while she convalesced from her souse. The ingredients, the utensils, and the charcoal *brasero* were novel to me. Fresh meat was a luxury in that isolated spot—it had to be killed and eaten in a day, hence our *pièce de résistance* consisted of *carne seca*, leathery dried goat meat, covered with chili gravy. We never pretended to swallow it out of deference to our innards; we only sucked off the chili gravy and removed the rest in the best-bred manner possible. I tackled one of these sheets of hide only to discover that a razor edged knife made not the slightest impression on it. I was utterly baffled, never having seen our *cocinera* [cook] as she hacked it in shreds with one sharp stone over a larger one. I fared no better with the *fideo*, a kind of Mexican spaghetti, and when my lord and master appeared on the scene, he discovered the impromptu cook in tears. We retired hungry.

---

1. Liquor made from the prickly maguey plant which grows in many parts of Mexico. There is a saying, *"para todo mal, mezcal, y para todo bien también"* (for everything bad, mezcal, and for everything good, as well).

18

Artist's romantic portrait of a *mozo*.

Upon arousing from my siesta in the late afternoon of the day that followed, I was greeted by a vile odor which seemed to have its origin in the rear of the house. This was not an unusual thing in this section where ice and cellars are unknown, but perhaps because of the stifling heat to which I was not accustomed, it became intolerably obnoxious. Gathering courage, I proceeded to Chelina's realm to investigate. Great was the offense to my nostrils, but greater still the offense to my vision when I gazed upon the contents of a simmering pot. In addition to the disjointed sections of the petrified carcass of a chicken, I beheld the feathered head, the unskinned feet, and the entrails, with a few things I couldn't identify thrown in for good measure. Beyond any doubt, she had picked up this fowl many hours after its demise. A dead chicken was a dead chicken to Chelina; of what moment to her the time and manner of its death? Not for an instant did I believe that she had intended this savory dish for our table. Nevertheless, I felt outraged that my home should be filled with the stench of it. Any lingering fear took flight, and with the supreme arrogance and tactlessness of youth, I consigned Chelina's feast to the garbage pail. She stood silent and motionless except for the quivering of her sunken lips. Once I had the impression that she muttered something inaudibly. Did this animated little mummy breathe a curse on me? Could the mishaps that have befallen me be traced to the witch-like concoction and my heartlessness? Who knows?

Portrait:
Mrs. Finnegan

Life had been damnably serious; I had forgotten what it was to laugh heartily when Mrs. Finnegan crossed my path. She was as good as a tonic. Her heart was warm and elastic; room enough there for all mankind. The really handsome black eyes that flashed fire one moment were apt to be moist with tears the next. Fat and soft in body, but sharp in tongue, her philosophy of life was unique, and what she could do with the King's English was amazing. She held me spellbound. She seemed to get the keenest zest out of living when sparring with her spouse; notwithstanding his twenty years under the Stars and Stripes, Finnegan was as Irish as his name, but his wits couldn't keep pace with hers. He was the bull's-eye for all her shafts, good natured or scathing according to her need. Not until he retired in defeat behind the bulwark of the *Daily News* did the barrage cease. Seeing him cowed, she seemed to relent and, with arms akimbo, would sigh: "Ah, well, Finnegan, he have his good pints and he have his bad pints." With that, I knew the comedy was over and the curtain down.

But the cruel hand of destiny reached down and struck a death blow to this dear old lady. Lillian, her heart's pride, the very center of her universe, was crushed under a modern Juggernaut while hurrying to her work with her Mother's kiss still warm on her lips. Surely this couldn't be real? Such ghastly tragedies as this belong to the movies; they don't come home to us in this fashion.

Broken in body and mind, my little Irish friend passed beyond my horizon.

Portrait:
The Sainting of a Sinner

Late in the afternoon of a dry, scorching day in midsummer, I emerged from the *zaguán* [hall] door and gazed about disconsolately. Nothing to be seen in any direction but the squatty mud houses and *tiendas* [shops], with a sprinkling of indolent natives sprawled about, some dozing, some smoking the interminable *cigaros*. Beyond this, the great barren stretches of sun-baked sand from which the heat waves rose in a dozy haze.

I was all dressed up, but obviously there was no place to go. Our stay in this tiny Mexican hamlet had been unexpectedly prolonged. Anything that had seemed picturesque upon arrival had long since become sordid and unlovely; I had tasted too much of the discomfort and loneliness of isolation. With no particular objective, I meandered down the street, wobbling over the cobblestones as I shooed scrawny chickens, skinny dogs, and half-naked children out of my path of progress.

Turning a corner, my attention was arrested by two approaching female figures. They were neither more nor less ragged than those of the village, but something in their appearance and manner revealed that they were strangers from some remote spot still further in the interior. By the time I reached this conclusion, they had drawn near, and I became conscious that their attention was also riveted on me. The brown eyes of the child opened wide, and, for a moment, she paused, gazing in silent awe.

Then swiftly she ran to me and, with clasped hands and frequent glances heavenward, burst into a torrent of adoration, at intervals touching with reverent fingers my hair, my skin, my garments. My knowledge of her language was most limited at that time, but I caught such flattering terms as "angel," "white dove," "most beautiful" and many other attributes that never before or since were bestowed upon me. I grasped the truth: for the first time in her life, this child had seen a white woman, a blue-eyed blonde at that. When she fell on her knees at my feet and literally kissed the hem of my skirt, I wanted to turn and run. I possessed a normal quota of the vanity of youth, but such extravagant and unmerited homage as this was overwhelming and embarrassing.

Suddenly the pathos of the situation gripped me. How bleak and barren of beauty must have been the life of this starved little soul that a commonplace woman in a simple white linen frock should seem to her a celestial, glorified being! Even Nature had cheated her with its interminable stretches of sand and cactus.

What could I do to disillusion this little maid and to convince her that I was of the earth and earthy? Perhaps my husky young infant would prove to her that I was an ordinary mortal. Hopefully, I led them to my quarters and produced my bouncing boy. Lo, I became a Madonna and this snub-nosed, pink-faced babe, a cherub, adorned with halos. 'Twas no use; I gave up. After filling them with rapture and Yankee ambrosia, I sent them on their way, knowing full well that I had been sainted in spite of honest efforts to remain a sinner.

Portrait:
Sara Hubbard

The telephone rang, and a pleasant, mellow voice asked permission to call and interview me in regard to my "Cook Wanted" in the morning paper. Answering the doorbell an hour later, I stared in amazement at what I beheld; here was a veritable mountain of black flesh; never had I seen anything so prodigious belonging to the human species. I doubt if a penny-in-the-slot machine could have measured her bulk. She was clean, but ragged, hatless, and bare of legs, though her huge feet were covered with black bedroom slippers. Around one ankle she wore a pierced dime on a shoestring—a charm guaranteed to prevent rheumatism.

Recovering my lost speech, I inquired if it was she who had talked with me.

"Yassum, I'se Sara Hubbard; I'se a good cook, and I wants a job."

I hesitated in embarrassment; how should I handle this situation? I had encouraged her to come to see me, but obviously she was impossible. Then I remembered the pile of unwashed dishes in the sink and the uncooked dinner. Opening the screen that had separated us, I invited her to come in and go to work, with the mental reservation that she should go when a more promising candidate appeared.

With difficulty she squeezed through the door from which she was not to make a permanent exit for three years. Before a suitable rival presented herself, Sara had made a tremendous appeal to our affections as well as to our appetites. She was one of those rare treasures, "an old timey niggah." She took a personal and proprietary interest in our affairs; she loved to help me dress for any special occasion and watched with beaming family-pride when I sallied forth attractively gowned.

Sara had the passionate love of music and rhythm characteristic of her race; more than once I returned home to find her enthralled at the player piano, pumping away with a zeal that threatened to burst the bellows. But the rolls we had selected as a part of the musical education of our offspring failed to satisfy her yearnings; Sara and Beethoven didn't vibrate on the same piano; she craved the "Yellow Dog Blues" and similar classics, and I felt she had a right to choose her own soul's music nourishment, provided she did her feasting during our absences.

Sara was not without her imperfections; occasionally I caught her slipping one of her delicious lemon pies or some other delicacy to her numerous lady and "genman" friends who called at her quarters apart from the house; but long since had I learned that one must be oblivious to many such things. Their code of ethics did not forbid such hospitality at another's expense, and one must accept it or remain cookless. She became momentarily sulky when reproved, but there was never any hint of any serious undercurrent of sullenness. Her flashing smile was contagious, and her rich, vibrant, good-natured laugh was worth traveling to hear. Yet, sometimes when she thought herself alone, she crooned weird, unearthly, tuneless chants with an indescribable savage note that fairly congealed my blood. She carried me to distant Africa, and I had visions of her ancestors making preparation to feast on one of mine.

The months slipped by—nearly thirty-six of them—before anything occurred to upset our domestic peace; then, suddenly, it dawned on me that Sara was unusually silent as she went about her duties; closer attention revealed that she was looking worn and worried. As tactfully as possible, I tried to learn what was troubling her; she insisted that all was well so I let it pass until I discovered a wicked jackknife with a broad six-inch blade on the piano. She admitted it was hers, but would give no explanation concerning it. This set me thinking; I had lived for many years in the Sunny South and knew something of the personal lives of some of her people, but Sara—ah, no, she was different; it was unthinkable that she should have vicious intentions.

Some days later, I awoke to find the kitchen deserted and no breakfast in sight. A peep into Sara's room showed a bed in which no one had slept the night before. I was puzzled, then anxious. I went to the telephone.

"Yassum, this is Susie; No'm, sistah won't be theah no moah; she got jealous of a woman who tried to take her man away; last night at a dance she slashed her with a knife and they done took her to jail."

Thus Sara made her exit!

A typical Mexican cook preparing a meal.

Portrait: Maria

Maria was a dainty thing. My attention was focused particularly on her exquisite little hands as they fluttered with movements among the pots and pans. My own hands, though white, soft, and pink-nailed, were large, strong, and plebian by comparison. Sometimes I grew meditative, rather uncomfortably so, as I watched her. Who was I and through what series of events and processes of evolution was I to sit in lazy contemplation while this tiny brown-skinned creature performed the menial and sometimes heavy tasks that contributed to my comfort?

Like most of her kind, Maria was appallingly ignorant, but unlike the others, her mind was alert and hungry. I learned that her universe was bounded on the East by Mexico, on the South by Mexico, on the West by Mexico, and on the North by— Texas. She questioned me exhaustively on this topic. Seeking to enlarge her horizon somewhat, I brought the boys' little globe; it only filled her with paralyzed bewilderment. I remembered her religion. Moving my pencil across the seas, I said, "Maria, you have heard of Italy, haven't you?" Her little brow puckered in intense concentration. "Ah, yes, *Señora*, Italy is in Rome where lives the Holy Father."

My baubles were safe; not for worlds would Maria have touched them except to admire. But the medicine chest—that was another story; she had a mania for sampling anything in a bottle, and the rather complete assortment of remedies we found necessary in that isolated spot drew her like a magnet. On one occasion she became really ill. Calling me to her room, she announced gravely and dramatically that she was going to die. It distressed her to cause me so much trouble, but would I be so gracious as to send for her uncle, her only near relative, who was a *mozo* in a neighboring village.

Diagnosing her affliction as a violent attack of biliousness, I suggested a home remedy while we waited for the priest, the doctor, and the uncle. She watched it effervesce in fascination and drank it eagerly, expectantly. But, alas, the sick and outraged little stomach would have none of it; it was immediately expelled to the great discomfort of both the patient and the nurse. Much against my liking, I had to bully the gentle soul into giving a second one a trial. Several hours later, I entered the room just as she awoke from a long sleep. I inquired after her present state of health. With eloquence of voice, hands, and shoulders, she informed me that, through the great favor of God and my remedies, she was relieved.

Maria had a twelve-year-old offspring. Juanita was a lively, noisy youngster who had a bad habit of racing hilariously around the house during siesta hour. The head of the household protested, and I became the go-between. Maria was genuinely distressed and promised to subdue the exuberant spirits of her angel child. Several days elapsed with no improvement, and I was forced to speak to her once more, this time rather sternly. Never shall I forget the pained look on that expressive little face as she explained to me that, much as it grieved her to so molest the *Señor*, she dare not punish this child—"Why, *Señora*, she is the daughter of Don Juan Fernandez," she added in a tone of mingled pride and awe. Not one word of bitterness or rebellion over the long years of toil and self-sacrifice that fell to her lot. Her expression changed to one of dreamy rapture and exaltation. She had been honored and set apart from the common herd by this great man's fleeting attention.

I was silenced. In the stormy years of the Revolution that followed, we sailed for a safe port. What of Maria and the sacred child?

The Mexican Revolution began with random uprisings in 1910, protests against foreigners growing rich on the resources of the nation while the average Mexican lived in dire poverty. Unrest continued to escalate, but Margaret's husband refused to leave Mexico. In 1913, as the crisis worsened, their eldest son, now seven, was put on a train alone, with the hope he would reach safety in Texas. Margaret and her four-year-old son stayed behind with her husband. One night early in 1915, the call came that the local guards had deserted the American compounds and revolutionary troops were just a few miles away.

My Last Day on Foreign Soil

Affairs had reached an acute stage in the revolution south of the Rio Grande. Soldiers and *"soldadas,"* as their accompanying females were called, were in tatters and near starvation. Thousands of *peóns* who had gone into the army in a rather good-natured spirit of adventure were now becoming ugly and aggressive toward non-combatants. The hills that flanked the fertile acres of Tlahualilo Plantation made a perfect fortress for the straggling bands who were now taking on the habits of bandits. There they could abide in safety until the time was ripe to make a swoop.

Late one stormy night a voice called up from the patio of *La Casa Grande:* "For God's sake, come down here, and hurry. Mañuel has telephoned from Hacienda Cordova that the bandits are headed this way, and the guard is deserting."

The guard leaving us! The two-hundred armed, well-fed, and well-paid men who had given us such a sense of security! But why expect loyalty from a mere handful of men when whole armies flocked cheerfully from one General to his enemy if it seemed to promise any personal advantage?

33

With frantic haste we donned what garments were at hand, chucked a few indispensables into a bag, and joined the other members of the colony below. Thirteen of us—ye gods—and our baggage to crowd into three cars for a runaway jaunt to the nearest point of safety.

It fell to the lot of me and mine to occupy the one on which the lights were out of commission. The sandy soil had been washed into deep gullies by the heavy downpours of the rainy season, and we lurched drunkenly from side to side with only the frequent flashes of lightening to save us from disaster.

Forty tense, endless miles before we reached our destination, only to learn from a faithful native employee that we escaped the bandits by a margin of thirty minutes. They amused themselves by looting our homes and other buildings. What could not be carried away was destroyed. Members of the former guard who had joined forces with them were recognized days later, auctioning off our clothing and other more valuable belongings.

Pancho Villa and *Villistas*

Similar experiences were being enacted in various parts of the country. Foreign lives were no longer safe, and women and children were straggling in from every point of the compass. An urgent call from the President of the U.S.A. besought the citizens of his nation to return to the fold, but we responded with reluctant feet, finding it hard to pull up the roots so deeply implanted in Mexico's soil.

A refugee train was organized: a ludicrous mixture of passenger and freight cars. Traveling had become hazardous. Many miles of track had been burned, and the rails had been hurriedly placed with practically no ballast. A headlight would attract too much attention, so we rocked dangerously along, with only a torch attached to the cow-catcher to light our way.

Women and children and babies! Flies, fleas, heat, the stench of sweaty bodies and stale food! Bridges had been dynamited, and detours were forced, making interminable a journey between two points that could normally be covered in forty-eight hours.

On our third day en route, we suddenly heard the whine of rifle shots and felt the thud of bullets on the walls of the cars. A cry went up that the bandits were approaching, and instantly the air was filled with shrieks. The woman who sat by me nursing her infant fainted straight-away, forcing me into composed action that I could not otherwise have achieved. Perhaps my Quaker blood served me in good stead in this crucial moment. I took the baby from her arms and dropped to the floor below the window, dragging the mother with us, and there we lay huddled while the train increased its speed in a mad flight in which the element of danger was quite as great as that from which we fled.

Presently I became detached and utterly calm. I recalled a roll of bills and trinkets concealed on my person which I removed and hid in the unused cuspidor, humorously determined that if I couldn't have them, no one else should either.

A refugee train escaping the revolutionaries.

But the end was not to be! We soon out-distanced them without a single casualty, and, within a few hours, only damaged window panes and shocked nerves remained as evidence of our narrow escape. The rest of the journey was uneventful, though it was the very essence of discomfort and fatigue. Stops were infrequent and uncertain, and quite as often were made in some isolated, barren spot as elsewhere. Our supply of water must therefore be carefully husbanded; it was an unwritten law that it must be used only to quench our thirst and cook our food, and sparingly at that.

But I was young and selfish. My natural fastidiousness was outraged by a heavy coating of sweat, dust, and cinders. On one occasion I sneaked into the tiny wash-room and stealthily put two or three cups of the precious liquid into the bowl. I was about to submerge my hands when the train gave an unusually wicked lurch and splattered the contents all over my clothing. My sin had found me out. I could not remain concealed until dry and so stood convicted on sight!

We passed through endless miles of sand, cactus, and sage-brush, of desolation and destruction. The weary monotony of this passing landscape was occasionally relieved by some gruesome aftermath of the local conflict. Bloated bodies hung stark and purple from telegraph poles, looking like scarecrows or effigies.

At the close of our fifth day, we found ourselves out of danger, but deep in trouble. American customs officials looked with suspicion on such a haggard, disreputable bunch. Instead of a

36

hearty, brass band welcome back to "God's Country," we were ordered in a peremptory and unChristian manner to strip to the skin. While our already bedraggled garments were tied into huge bundles and baked in an oven, we were initiated into the fragrant delights of a gasoline bath. Not a hair of our heads was overlooked.

With diminishing regret, we said our final *adios* to the sand, cactus, heat, fleas, chili, and bandits of the land of *"La Mañana."*

Margaret and son in Texas.

Here, there is nearly a decade's gap in the surviving manuscripts. Either she stopped writing or the drafts were lost in the turmoil that followed. Revolution in Mexico ended, but not the revolution in her life.

During the fighting, she and her two boys waited in San Antonio for her husband to join them. Years passed, and his love letters, starting "Dearest Girl" and "Sweetheart," were carefully preserved. In June of 1917, he was ready to join her, but cancelled at the last minute for business reasons. His letters became more distant.

He arrived in San Antonio in December, there was a bitter and explosive encounter, and they were divorced a few weeks later in January 1918. Two weeks after that, he wrote: "It completely slipped my mind to leave you any money." A few months later, he married a woman nearly half his age.

Now thirty-six years old, she found herself alone with two children, no marketable job skills, and the added social stigma of divorce. Her former husband rarely responded to her letters pleading for support or had any contact with his children. Her next recorded adventure finds her in Manhattan, far from the Sonoran desert.

A Taste of Inferno

The famous Neurologist delivered his ultimatum in a calm, casual manner, not knowing that it brought my whole world tumbling about my head. A complete rest and change of environment for an indefinite period, that was all he asked.

For ten years I had been battling to fill the elemental and educational needs of my two young sons. An unforeseen personal tragedy had forced me out of my feathered nest, entirely unprepared to use my own wings. The long period of sorrow, anxiety, and grinding toil had undermined my health. I had overdrawn my account with Nature, and she had come to collect.

My low, involuntary moan brought the doctor's searching glance to my colorless, haggard face. "If you are without funds, Mrs. K——, I think I can find a way to help you, but I must ask you to enter the hospital for a period of observation before further steps can be taken." This sentence added humiliation to the rest of my misery. I had confessed that I had not known one hour of natural sleep for many months. I understood the purpose of this period of surveillance; he must be certain that it was only Veronal[1] and not a narcotic that I had used as a temporary relief. I had reached the bottom of my resources; there was nothing to do but to submit, though I felt it might cost my sanity.

On a bleak, bitter day in February, I entered a ward in old Bellevue Hospital. When I was wheeled into the room, the head nurse asked crisply: "Well, what's the matter with you?" Upon being told that I was suffering from a nervous collapse, she exclaimed to the nurse who had ushered me in: "Well, I'll be damned. What did they send her in here for?"

Before I left the institution, I learned to respect that over-worked, sorely-tried woman. The rough speech and hard exterior hid a big heart. I learned, too, the cause of her wrath that had hurt me so cruelly at my arrival.

Bellevue Hospital, New York City, 1920

The ward which was meant for about twenty-four was already accommodating thirty. The beds were crowded closely together, and cots were lined up in the center of the room. The congestion

---

1. Veronal is a brand name for the barbiturate Barbital, a sedative-hypnotic used for sleep. It is not, pharmacologically or legally, a narcotic, but today it is a controlled substance, infrequently prescribed.

made it difficult to get anything done, and, in many ways, overtaxed the time and strength of her very limited corps of nurses.

I was led to a cot, given a huge, coarse nightgown, and told to disrobe. One of the probationers made a hurried, half-hearted attempt at placing a screen about me, but it proved to be wholly inadequate. Two-thirds of the patients had an unobstructed view if they were interested. Bitter poverty has brought so many shocks to my sensitive nature that I have since become "sensible," but at that time I shrank in torture from this exposure.

The high, barn-like room was draughty and the bedding scanty. By the time the young intern paid his first visit to my bedside, I was shaking with cold and nervousness. "Doctor," I said, "I am cold."

He answered bluntly, "So am I." I glanced at his white linen suit and believed that he told the truth.

After a pause, I asked timidly, "May I please have another blanket or a hot-water bottle?"

"If I ordered a blanket or a hot water bottle for you, every woman in this ward would howl for the same," I was told. I couldn't know that he was getting only four or five hours of sleep out of the twenty-four of ceaseless duty, and that he was harassed by countless unreasonable requests from the patients. I subsided into dumb misery. Later, I became crafty. The nurse did not approve of disarranged beds, so I surreptitiously smuggled a warm bathrobe down under the covers, close to my thin, under-nourished little body.

The situation among these submerged human derelicts was not wholly without humor. My neighbor on the right was a huge person who could scarcely move without assistance. One day, I heard her groaning and puffing while her face turned crimson and wet from exertion. She was obviously trying to reach over the edge of her high bed for something she had dropped.

I discovered a small bottle of forbidden medicine which had slipped away from her. Pet remedies were frequently smuggled in by well-intentioned friends. She was profusely grateful for the rescue, saying over and over: "Thank you, lady, thank you: My Gawd, what would Miss S_____ say if she had seen me?"

The neighbor on my left was uncommunicative. She would lie for hours in a kind of stupor; only at meal time did she show any animation. A special diet had been prescribed over which she complained, bitterly. On one occasion she covered herself with many layers of newspaper, left behind during visitors' hour. When asked why she did it she replied that her bowels were cold.

One tiny, little white-haired Irish ward-maid looked after the whole fretful bunch of us. She should have been tucked into one of the beds herself. Some of the patients slipped her a dime now and then, but I don't think she played any favorites. There were no bells to ring and no red lights to flash, only peevish or plaintive calls for "Mary, Mary" from all directions at once. Feeling grateful for her attention, I once remarked, "Mary, you're an angel."

"Huh, I don't see no wings asproutin'," she came back at me.

On about the third day, I found my body, and particularly my neck, well covered with red pimples. A young woman doctor, the aspiring daughter of a well-known New York man, had replaced the other intern. She wasn't weighed down with gray matter, but she had a heart, a thing not worn on the sleeve around Bellevue. She became very solicitous over my "skin affliction" and finally called in two consulting doctors, one of them a skin specialist. They held a learned conference at my bedside, using technical terms that conveyed nothing to the ears of a layman. Highly tense and rebellious over the whole situation, I finally burst out: "Well, if a mere patient dare express an opinion, I think it is bedbugs." There was a moment of dead silence; I could have bitten my tongue out when I saw the flush of embarrassment on my doctor's face. Then the men began to laugh heartily. The specialist said: "Why, you don't think they have bedbugs in Bellevue, do you?"

"How could they help it, with all the riff-raff that is brought in here?" I answered. Thus ended the examination. Within an hour, a man with a big tank of ill-smelling exterminating liquid came in with a pump and sprayed both me and the bed, though I was probably not intentionally included.

In the bed facing mine from across the room lay a very young girl, plump, bright-eyed and fresh-faced. Since she showed no trace of illness I decided that she must have been injured until I noticed that she put on slippers and moved quietly around when she cared to. Although I was a very sick, despondent woman, my condition never completely submerged my natural interest in my fellow beings.

Bellevue Hospital, New York City

I made inquiry of my nurse and learned that she was an "interesting" case: a cardiac. We later became friendly, and I uncovered gradually what seemed to me a real tragedy. From early childhood, she had been told by some city physician that she had a bad heart, and that she must be very, very careful and not do any of the things that the other children did. Her loving, widowed mother had unwittingly fostered her fear until, at seventeen, Harriet had developed into a mental case. She had the movements of a decrepit old lady, walking as though each step might prove to be her last. She was intelligent and shrewd. Her natural indolence had developed into something colossal. Hearing her doctor talk of the heart building up "a compensation" under complete rest, she had frequent attacks that brought her to Bellevue for a period of idleness. Her mother needed her help economically. She had secured several openings in which the girl could have made a substantial contribution to the family budget without over-taxing the afflicted organ, but, no, when the novelty wore off she invariably suffered one of her spells and took another rest cure. The things from which most of us shrank in horror

43

filled Harriet with a morbid fascination. She would watch a dying woman until the very last gasp and be prepared to relate the gruesome details to any who would listen. Many times since I have wondered what fate held in store for that lovely, psychopathic young girl.

One day, shortly after I entered, I heard a hair-raising shriek; I turned a startled, inquiring face to the little nurse who was making up my bed. "That's one of the nuts in the Psychopathic Ward," she informed me. I was allowed to move about and soon became familiar with the faces at the window of this ward, which stood apart from the main building. Only the women were visible, but the men patients could be heard. I watched them in unhealthy absorption, wondering if I might not one day be among them.

One I called the Madonna. She had long, flowing hair and a lovely, refined face which was turned at frequent intervals to the Children's Ward above us. She crooned and called to them in piteous fashion, asking for her baby. Sometimes she burst into fervent prayer.

The one I called Old Mag used to push her aside, and then the air was filled with oaths, ribald songs, and coarse speech. She made hideous faces and did every indecent thing she could think of, looking furtively in the direction of the nurse from time to time, to avoid detection.

Then there was Flapper Ann who would put on a flower-bedecked hat, make up her face, and sit in the window, all dressed up with no place to go.

Among the men, one shell-shocked victim sang romantic songs in a mellow tenor. It pleased my fancy to visualize him as a handsome youth. He was often interrupted by an ex-teamster who gee'd and hawed his horses in a low bellow. Sometimes the sensitive singer would order him to shut up, bringing a stout "I won't" in reply, and the "Shut up" and the "I won'ts" would alternate ad infinitum, until the whole ward joined in the hideous din, making noise enough to awake the dead.

A pneumonia patient within fifteen feet of me lay dying. Her struggle for breath was a ghastly, terrible thing. My own condition had become more and more acute. Sensitively organized and almost abnormally sympathetic to pain in others, I had, in these surroundings, reached a stage of tension that was intolerable. I had begun to seek means of self-destruction when the incredible happened: the kind of thing that seems farfetched in fiction. The young doctor who had been in charge when I entered had returned to the ward. As I watched him making his rounds for the night, it suddenly flashed into my mind that the son of a dear friend had been in Bellevue for his internship. In the crowded, strenuous atmosphere of a great metropolis, one loses all track of time. I could not recall how long it had been since he was admitted, but some inner voice prompted me to ask: "Do you by any chance know a Doctor Fitch who was here sometime ago?"

"Fitch," he exclaimed, "do I know Fitch? Well, I should say I do. We were old classmates in college. He is still here and has a room just across the hall from me." My pulse began racing with excitement as I explained that I had known him since his kindergarten days. Later on, after the lights had been dimmed for the night, two men entered and came swiftly to my bed.

One of them dropped to his knees and encircled me with his arms. We were speechless for a time, Edward from astonishment and I from relief and thanksgiving. He had last seen me in my own beautiful home in the South. He couldn't grasp the fact that the vicissitudes of life had brought me to this. "Why, man," he said to his friend, "Mrs. K___ rocked me in my cradle."

Which was slightly inaccurate, but what did a few years more or less matter in such a crisis. I was quietly and speedily removed to a private room until my release and convalescence in a happier environment could be arranged.

Poor old Bellevue. Grand old Bellevue, groaning and fairly bursting under its burden of suffering humanity, I bear it no grudge. It does what it can to alleviate the wretchedness of Manhattan's teeming millions.

This poignant portrait shows she continued to analyze and chronicle other women and also suggests that she was involved in social work at one time.

May Baker – U.S.A.

Case No. 68 had many aliases, but in the office of the [Vice] Board she was familiarly known as May Baker. As ordinary citizens of a great commonwealth or as fathers of the human race, men may "live their own lives," but, as fodder for cannon, they must be kept in the pink. It was our duty, therefore, to make the lives of May and her ilk as miserable as possible for the protection of the flower of our manhood. In neatly arranged folders in our files were chronicled the sad histories of several hundred of her kind; some of them hated us cordially, others took May's generous, good-natured attitude: "Well, you're The Law; you've got your business and I've got mine; it's a game of hide and seek; catch me if you can." Under the inadequate laws of the state, the only penalty for being "caught" was a fine; if physically fit, they were released only to be dragged again at some later date before the courts, and thus the game went futilely on.

May called quite frequently, sometimes at our urgent request, on other occasions of her own volition. The facts of her life as we knew them, were infinitely tragic; begotten in crime and wretchedness, she was lured at a tender age into a den of iniquity where she was held in virtual slavery until all moral perception was hopelessly blunted. Those of us who walk the more sheltered paths of life think such stories the product of the fertile brain of the yellow novelist or of the dime movie; only those who come into close contact with submerged humanity learn that truth is verily more gruesome than fiction.

May found herself a fascinating topic; sordidly dramatic as were the facts, she drew lavishly on her vivid imagination in relating incidents of her life; No two versions were ever just the same. To put it gently, May was pathologically untruthful, but her lies were not only sly or cunning; with all the guilelessness of a child telling a fairy tale, she imparted dark secrets of her career—always in strictest confidence—and she believed them too. For the time being they were real to her.

One day she called, all in a flutter. A boy soldier from a neighboring camp had taken her to be his, for better or for worse. No shady, clandestine affair this—but a really, truly marriage. No blushing girl-bride ever trod the clouds in greater ecstasy than did May. She bubbled over with excitement.

The days and weeks passed in rapid succession in our busy quarters. Then came May once more, this time with a shadow on her face. It seemed that the newly acquired husband was insanely jealous and was destroying her happiness. I suggested as tactfully as possible that, under the circumstances, she must be very patient with him; it would take time to prove her loyalty. Tearful, but seemingly comforted, she went her way.

Then came the shock; May was murdered in a dance hall by the only man who had ever loved her, but who found the strain on his faith in her too great to bear. Diseased in body, subnormal in mind, and warped of soul, May was the product of men's sins "unto the third or fourth generation"; obviously she had never had a square deal in this life.

Our vigil over her was ended. How now about "The Law"? In the Court of Justice in the Great Beyond, what sentence will be pronounced? Released from the shackles of environment, will May's dwarfed soul be given a chance to grow?

Margaret, circa 1901

The internal references in this final story indicate it was written about 1924 when Margaret was forty-three years old. She speaks of seven years since the divorce (1917) and says that her children are still minors. Her eldest, born in 1904, would have been twenty.

The Heart Experience of an Obscure Woman

Brilliant and successful women are today turning the searchlight on their most intimate personal lives and fearlessly revealing to the public the things we endeavored for generations to conceal. Why are these confessions read with such avidity? Is it a somewhat morbid curiosity concerning the affairs of the shining ones, or does the answer lie in the universality of marital problems? What place in the scheme of things has the heart experience of the commonplace, obscure woman, one of the average who make up what might be called the backbone of our nation? To the sociologist, she is a "case" in the social structure, to her minister, she may be a discouraged sister in need of counsel; but for the thousands of readers of her own class and caliber, has her heart message any meaning or value?

My position as a wife seemed impregnable, and our relationship was in some respects unique. The seed of our affection was planted in kindergarten days. In later years, my husband told me of his first glimpse of me which was never erased from memory. The setting was not romantic. With my arms wrapped about two pickets of the fence that enclosed the large yard of our country home, I stood on a lower rail, peering through into the world that lay beyond. I was dressed in a Mother Hubbard—a garment unknown to the youngsters of the present generation—with two long pigtails hanging down my back and a sprinkling of freckles adorning my nose. His own appearance was equally free from the picturesque as he drove the family cow to a neighboring pasture. But, in that first exchange of glances, something happened. Let the mature, worldly-wise lover scoff in incredulity if he will; the fact remains unchanged that something definite, abiding, and vital entered our consciousness at that moment. Our first kiss was exchanged at the tender age of seven, and it wasn't given lightly. Throughout the years of adolescence, our lives touched at many points, and, as we grew in body and mind, our love kept pace. No definite proposal of marriage passed his lips, but at seventeen we found ourselves seriously planning our future together. We married during my husband's twenty-first year, his senior year in college, and learned the mysteries of sex life together, an experience as precious as it was unusual. A brother and sister of mine married a sister and brother of his, and in countless ways our lives seemed inextricably interwoven.

He was a big man, virile, magnetic, a He-man. He was by no means an Adonis, but was of a rugged, rather heroic mold, a sturdy-oak, dynamic type. Though he was absolutely devoid of any flirtatious proclivities, women adored him. I think his manners, the kind "made up of petty sacrifices,"[1] were his chief charm. They were not the result of training alone, but sprang from an innate breeding and thoughtful concern for the welfare of others. He had the gift of unostentatiously doing and saying just the right thing at the right time in the right way. To no man could the phrase "generous to a fault" be more aptly applied. What he possessed had no value to him except as it contributed to the comfort and well-being of those he

---

1. Ralph Waldo Emerson

"A big man, virile, magnetic." Her husband, far right.

loved. I want to stress this point of character which makes what followed so incredible.

His chief imperfection was a wicked temper which erupted at the most unexpected times and places. Strange to say, I never witnessed any exhibition of this during all those years of close association; apparently it had lain dormant during carefree youth and cropped out under the pressure and strain of later responsibilities.

Though the incident was of great import to me at the time, I now recall with amusement the first outburst that dimmed our bliss for the moment. The initial effort in his profession of mining engineer took us to a small coal mining camp in the midwest where the inhabitants and customs were quite as foreign to us as anything across the seas. Our first nest was a two-room shack with boarded up, unplastered walls. It had been carelessly papered, and wide, unsightly cracks ran with regularity from floor to ceiling. The college pennants, numerous pictures, and various decorations could not conceal these blemishes, which became a source of some acute offense to us.

In an inspired moment, we conceived the idea of repapering it ourselves; it looked simple, and youth is so confident. Alas, we were to discover that even paperhanging has its techniques. The first covering of cheesecloth behaved quite decently, and even the paper on the side walls yielded to persuasion and stuck, but the ceiling—there we met our Waterloo; by the time we reached the end of one strip, the other half had peeled off and dangled in mid-air; we determinedly joked about it for a time, but presently I saw my husband's mouth grow grim and his eyes steely, presaging the outburst of wrath that followed. The outpouring of raw, sulfuric oaths blistered my young Quaker ears; it was a revelation to me. I had never heard anything that even approached it in my life. "My crickety" was the most vehement ejaculation in the vocabulary of my gentle old Dad, and this was uttered only under severe provocation.

When a Welsh neighbor woman came to our rescue, adding a portion of glue to the paste and finishing the job with a triumphant flourish, my husband's good humor was instantly restored. These brain storms seemed to clear the atmosphere as far as he was concerned; there was no lingering murkiness or sullenness. For me, the effect was more lasting, not because of any petty pouting, but for reasons of temperament. The shock of violence of word or deed brought a physical and mental reaction that was entirely beyond my control and left me shaken and depressed.

Margaret (with glasses)

I was tiny, sensitively organized, appealing—they said. Intellectually, I was my husband's inferior; I didn't think. I vibrated. I had just enough of the artistic spark to bedevil me without bearing fruitful result, yet it served to keep me from being drab and boresome. In the riper wisdom of my mature years, I can, of course, see many ways in which I erred; it seems to me that I was appallingly ignorant and undeveloped. Some of my shortcomings were those common to youth in general, but others were more peculiarly my own. My besetting sin was extravagance; I had not the remotest conception of the worth of a dollar or the meaning of the toil behind the possession. My father had acquired wealth through pioneer investments in the mid-west, and, from childhood, I had been accustomed to what were luxuries in that little corner of the world. Mother was a confirmed invalid who followed the line of least resistance as a matter of self-preservation; hence, I went my own sweet way, visiting shops and dressmakers when the spirit moved me, and Father paid the bills without a murmur.

I sincerely tried to be careful in my expenditures during our marriage, but money simply oozed through my fingers, and I never had the slightest idea what had become of it. This sin has been expiated, heaven knows, in these last years of penury.

After the coming of the youngsters, my health was never robust and sometimes there were long intervals of discomfort and semi-invalidism. Women who are never really well learn to bear pain silently. I determined in the beginning that I was not going to be a whining, complaining wife and mother, and I never was, yet I was restricted in many ways that could but react on the family. I was, for instance, sometimes unable to participate in some event to which we had long looked forward, or perhaps I would be compelled to leave some pleasant social occasion when things were at their merriest. I was not unreasonable enough to expect my husband to hold himself within my limitations, but he did so of his own volition. Never did he utter an impatient word concerning this phase of our life, and, though I was receptive to the point of being clairvoyant at times, I never sensed any inward rebellion over any inconvenience or disappointment arising from my handicap. His conduct has since been cruel and even criminal, yet a flood of tenderness surges through me at the memory of that fineness. Yet, he didn't pamper me where I didn't need it. He was inclined to be short and crisp in speech, and his ready wit often carried a barb. I had sprung from a Quaker family who handled each other with gloves, but I learned that his hardier give-and-take was much more sensible and comfortable to live with.

Notwithstanding our frequent sparring and an occasional important difference to be adjusted, our comradeship throughout the early years was a delightful compound of serious mutual interests, fun, humor, and sympathy, and we were, on the whole, spontaneously and genuinely happy.

My first serious rival was not a woman, but a Republic. We had taken deep root on a cotton plantation south of the Rio Grande, and, with the coming of the revolution in that unfortunate little country, storm clouds began to develop on our own domestic sky. Separations of varying lengths were now forced upon us, and the intervals between contacts grew longer as the years passed. I made earnest effort to remain at his side, but after several harrowing encounters with bandits I was compelled to definitely withdraw for the safety and welfare of our two small sons. One season of eight months elapsed when communication of all kind was interrupted with his section of the country. This was the thin wedge that began to separate our thoughts and interests. With prophetic vision of the ultimate outcome, I besought him to make the necessary material sacrifices and join his little family, but he stuck stoically and stubbornly to his post, honest in the conviction that it was for our best good for him to do so.

Then along came the other woman, one of those consolers of lonely men. She was a divorcée seventeen years his junior. My own ability to appraise her accurately and dispassionately might be questioned under the circumstances, but it was the common consensus among our friends that the thing was a ghastly mistake. Had she been a woman of character and firm intelligence who could have held him and developed the best in him, the hurt and humiliation might have been less poignant, but she was just warm flesh and blood. The gall of my Gethsemane was the fact that he did for her what he had steadfastly refused to do for us—he left the danger zone and took up life anew where men could lie down on their beds at night with reasonable assurance that their heads would be still on their shoulders in the morning. Retribution was swift and sure. Hardly had they passed through the orthodox honeymoon before rumors were afloat that something was amiss. The sudden severing of all business and social ties brought unforeseen economic problems; they drifted hither and thither without getting a successful foothold. The quality of the tie between them was not of a fiber to withstand this test, and, after four years of squabbling and recriminations, they were legally separated.

But the sins of the father were visited upon the sons and their mother. Though born and reared in a well-feathered nest, I was compelled in my mature years to face the bread and butter question for myself and children. The years that followed were filled with cruel poverty, loneliness, ill health, and grim struggle. In my impotence, I groped for a higher, unseen Power and gained a knowledge of spiritual forces and values worth the price I paid for it. It carried me victoriously through untold hardships into comparative comfort and peace. This quickening of the soul put me in tune with the infinite and enabled me to reach a spiritual zenith.

The two lads who were in the beginning my liabilities have become my richest assets, and the closeness of the mother-and-son tie has never been surpassed. Though the elder is still a minor, he has, against tremendous odds, achieved marked distinction, both in the classroom and in the field of his chosen profession. The younger, too, is full of promise and has many of those little victories to his credit that fill the hearts of parents

Margaret with her first grandchild, Jim Knowles, 1931.

with pride. Only those happily mated ones who have together discussed and tenderly planned and dreamed dreams over the future of their offspring can understand what it means not to be able to share these little triumphs with the man who begot them.

Throughout these seven years, their father has maintained dismal silence, never in any way meeting his moral or financial obligation to them. The most staggering mystery of all has been this desertion of the boys he seemed to idolize. No children in this universe were more longed for and more deliberately brought into existence. Three years have now elapsed since the other woman passed beyond his horizon, yet he continues to shut them completely out of his life. This seems to me the very crest of the tragedy because it registers the depth of his soul slump. Remembering the warmth of his affection, the unselfish and thoughtful devotion, and the fine, generous spirit of his young manhood, the present situation seems unreal.

Two splendid men have paid me the tribute of their sincere love, yet never for more than a fleeting moment have I been tempted to mate with one to whom I could give only a fragment of my heart. I shall never know to just what degree I may have been responsible for this sad drama, but I am convinced that if I had clung to him through it all instead of demanding what I called "my freedom," harmony and trust and fondness would have been restored in due course. In my stupid blindness, I thought the severing of the legal bond would release his hold on my heart and alleviate my anguish, but I have never been able to let go. I rarely allow myself to deliberately contemplate the past; I know well the folly of that; yet, the wound has never healed. On every hand there are unavoidable reminders that bring a stab of pain at times, such as the extraordinary likeness of my firstborn to his sire, both of physiognomy and general characteristics.

To bare one's soul is futile and pointless unless there be a motive. My own purpose is to urge other women who may feel their foundations tottering to hold on resolutely. I am something of a feminist and an ardent advocate of the single standard all along the line, yet the older I grow, the more I realize that after all it is the woman who furnishes the key-note of the home, and that she must provide the ballast that steadies when things rock.

Men and women should learn to recognize these inevitable attractions between the sexes for the fleeting things they usually are and not allow them to disintegrate families and disrupt homes. Such associations, if disciplined into wholesome friendships minus the flirtatious notes, bring infinitely more enduring and richer returns. This is not a pious platitude, but psychological law. We are discovering that the "law of love" is a scientific law, and we cannot tamper with such and get away with it. I shall not launch into a tirade against the modern ideas of mating, but I will say that if they were followed out to their logical conclusion, the human race would soon be wallowing in a state of sordid and sensual promiscuity.

There is a good deal of bunkum in the talk of living one's own life. "No man living to himself alone"; others are always involved and the behavior of the individual, like the motion of the pebble tossed into the ocean, stretches across the entire sea of humanity. Marriage is fast becoming just a trial affair, entered into with mental reservations. There is not much of the "for better or for worse" spirit left, hence little honest effort is made to be mutually tolerant and forbearing. All attachments must be disciplined and spiritualized if they are to withstand the jar and fret of life. The emotional consciousness of love in any relationship fluctuates, whether it be that of mother and son, brother and sister, or man and wife. A waning of the warmth of this most intimate and vital of ties does not necessarily signify mismating or the final demise of the fondness that existed. Many couples who are going down the homestretch together successfully will confess that they faced intervals of indifference bordering perilously on dislike, only to see love burst into its fullest, most fragrant bloom after this cycle has passed.

How glorious the reward of the patience, insight, loyalty, and strength of our purpose that held the bond unbroken and inviolable!

Marguerite (Margaret) Loraine Heacock Knowles was born in Kingsley, Iowa on November 21, 1881 and died in Chicago, August 4, 1932, age fifty.

INDEX

Photos indicated by **bold face**

A Very Different Life is a publication of
Grand Cyrus Press, San Francisco.
To see other books in our catalogue, please visit
www.GrandCyrusPress.com

Grand Cyrus Press
Celebrating the Arts

www.ingramcontent.com/pod-product-compliance
Lightning Source LLC
Chambersburg PA
CBHW022131280326
41933CB00007B/644